Greece

Sacha de Frisching

Illustrations by Sylvie Rainaud

English edition prepared by Claudia Eilers

Originally published under the title
La Grèce en salopette by Hachette, Paris.

Photoset by Parker Typesetting Service, Leicester
Printed and bound in France by Offset Aubin, Poitiers

ISBN 0 330 29237 4

Whilst the advice and information in this book are believed to be true and accurate at the time of going to press, neither the author nor the publisher can accept any legal responsibility or liability for any errors or omissions that may be made

PICCOLO PICTURE BOOKS

Piccolo Globetrotters

Monastries of Metéora
Mount Athos
Lemnos
Corfu
Sporades
Lesbos
Ionian
Islands
Delphi
Athens
Corinth
Mycenae
Olympia
Epidaurus
Mykon
Delos
Naxos
Paros
Cyclades
Santorin
Yugoslavia
Bulgaria
Albania
Turkey
Crete

Land of 1000 islands: Greece

A scatter of mountains rising from the Mediterranean Sea – that's what most of Greece looks like: it has more than 1400 islands!

No wonder the Greeks have always been great sailors and navigators.

But Greece is also the ideal place for holidays in the sun and for discovering the ancient world.

Colour in the flags of all neighbouring countries, and then the Greek flag in the middle of the last row. If you look carefully you'll find it somewhere on this page.

Call of the sea

The winding Greek coastlines and countless islands mean that boats are the easiest means of transport. In the old days, travelling the seas was a real adventure and many legends relate the exploits of the great navigators.

Put the boats in order from the biggest to the smallest and you'll discover the name of a famous seafarer from antiquity.

Solution: Ulysses. For ten years he travelled the seas and his adventures are described by Homer in his poem called the 'Odyssey'.

The Greek merchant fleet is still one of the biggest in the world. In the empty boxes below, copy the drawings which correspond to each number and one of their huge ships will appear.

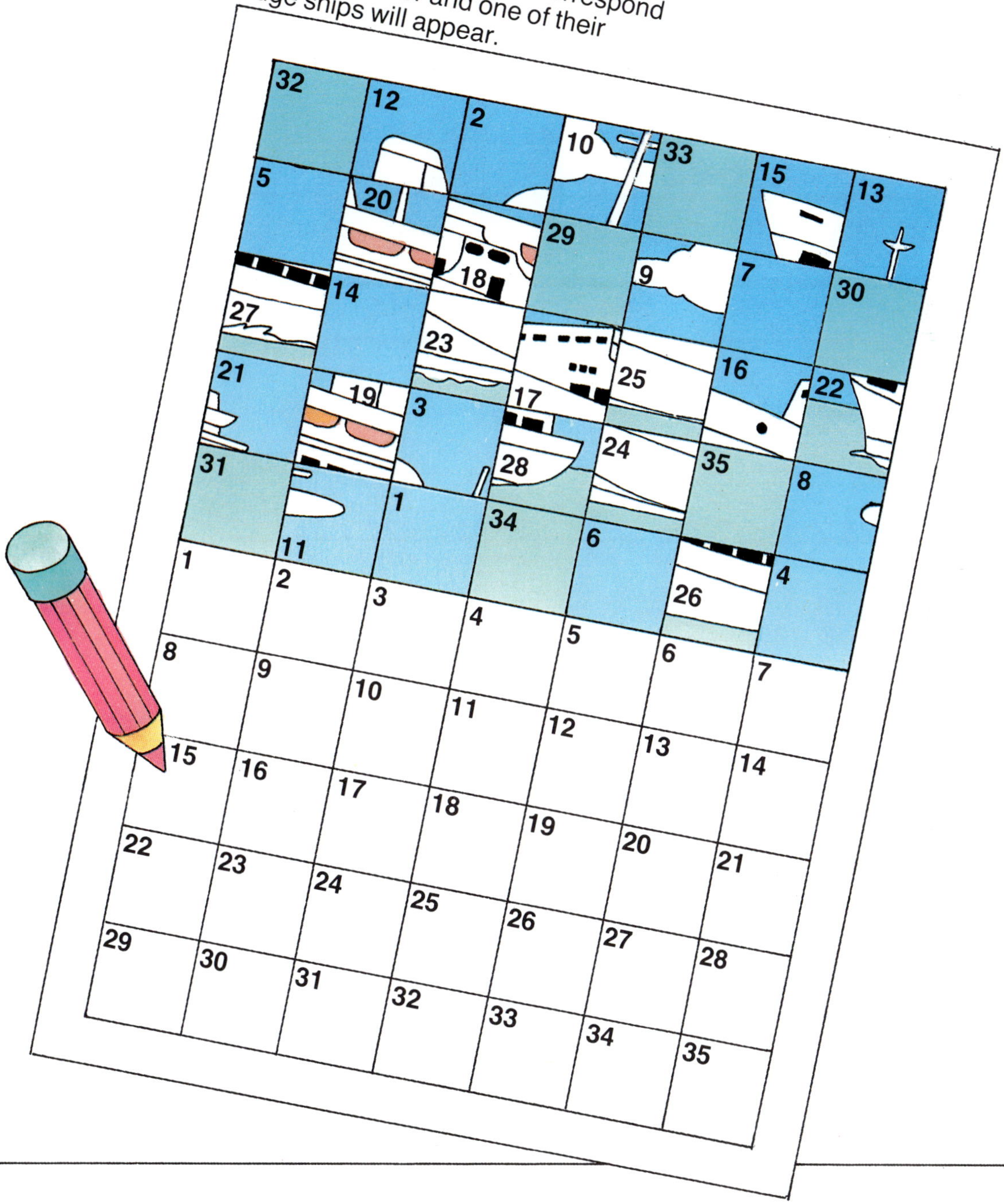

Sun-kissed

Greece is a sun-trap
and has the vegetation of
a hot and dry climate:
evergreen trees,
sweet smelling herbs
and fruit full of sugar.
Here are some typical plants,
their fruit and the products
made from them. Can you work out
which of these belong together?

Solution: Ac3; Ba1; Cb2; Dd4

One of these animals is not at home in Greece. Which one is it?

Solution: the reindeer

Alpha and Omega

The Greek alphabet is different from ours. Look at the capital letters below and pick up some Greek words by writing the corresponding letters into the yellow boxes.

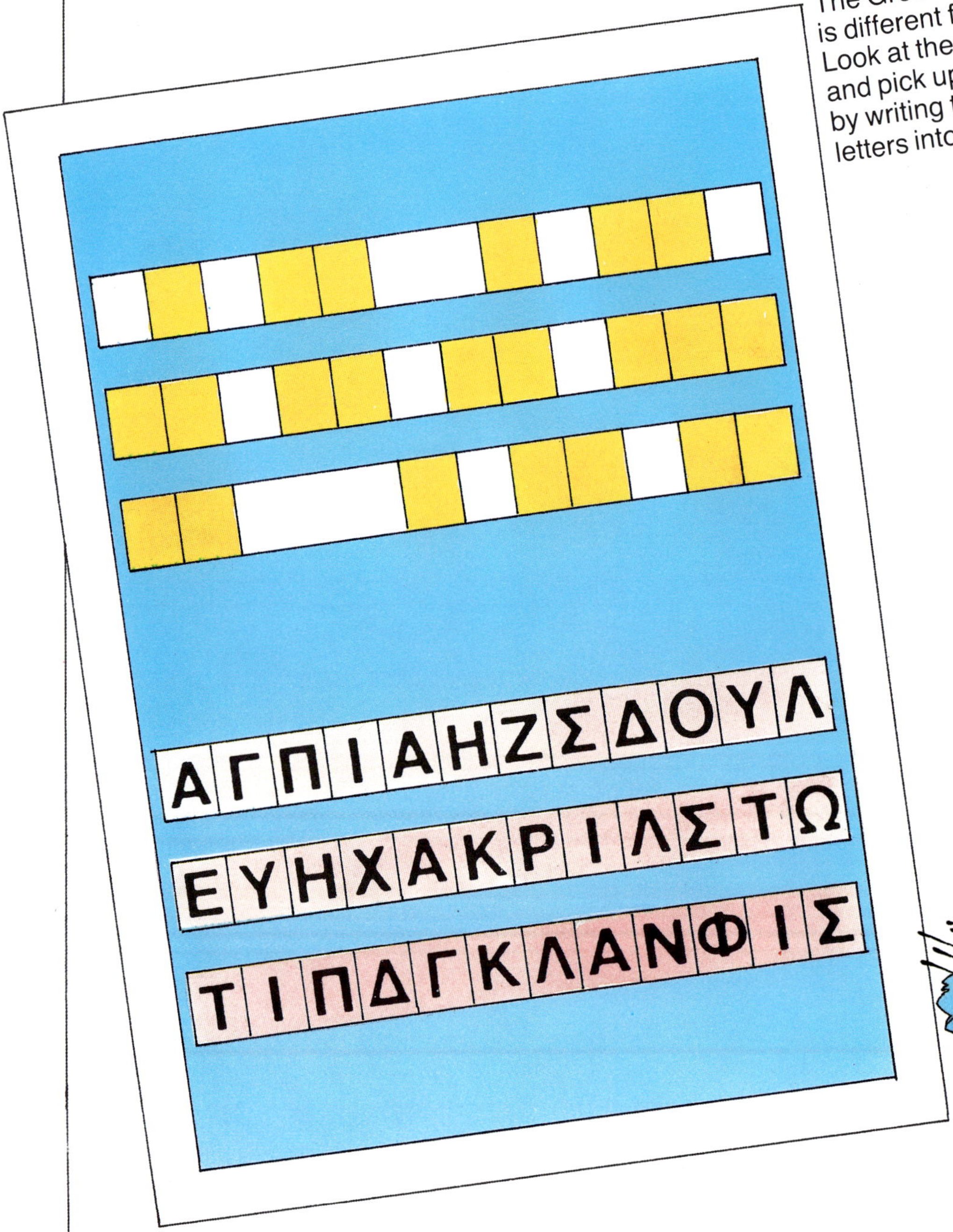

Solution: YIA SOU (hello!); EFHARISTO (thank you); TI KANIS (How are you?)

A genius

Arithmetic and geometry were developed in Ancient Greece and one of the greatest scholars was Archimedes. He is said to have made one of his discoveries . . . in his bath. His exclamation 'I've got it!' has become famous – in Greek, of course. You'll find the Greek word, if you put the letters in the red boxes in the right order.

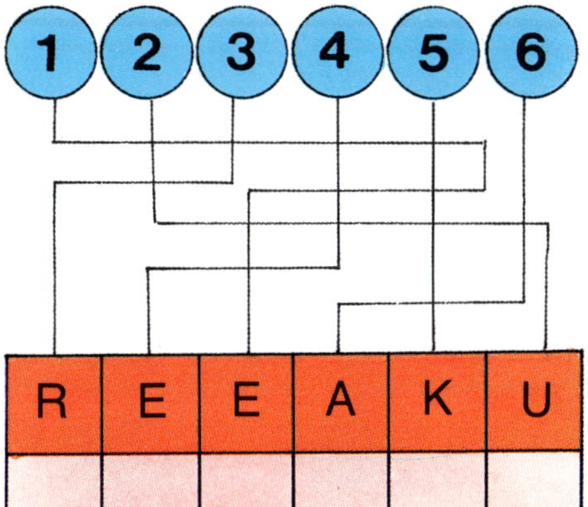

Olympic Games

Most of our present-day sports, especially athletics, were practised in Ancient Greece. All the young men trained for competitions and the best athletes gathered every four years for the celebrations in honour of the god Zeus, at Olympia. Our modern Olympic Games are modelled on those early sporting events.

I am preparing for the next Games.
Write the name for each sport
onto the pedestals.

What are the colours of the Olympic rings?
Find out from the previous page
and colour them in.

Solution: pole vault; high jump; discus throwing; shot putt; relay race; running.

Colossal columns

To honour their gods,
the Ancient Greeks built
sumptuous marble temples
and sculpted magnificent statues.
The style they created
has influenced architects
and artists ever since.
Study the columns on the next page and
decide what style this temple is.

Solution: Doric

There are three styles of Greek columns: study the top of each column in detail and you'll see the differences.
Now try to find the shortest route through this maze. You must follow the order: Doric, Ionic, Corinthian.

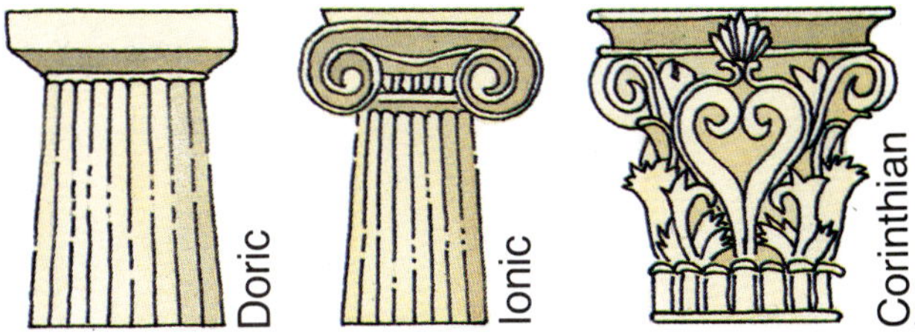

Start

Finish

In Ancient Greece, everyday objects such as oil-lamps, bowls, vases and toys were made from baked clay. The most beautiful ones were decorated and varnished. Be an archaeologist and fit the pieces together.

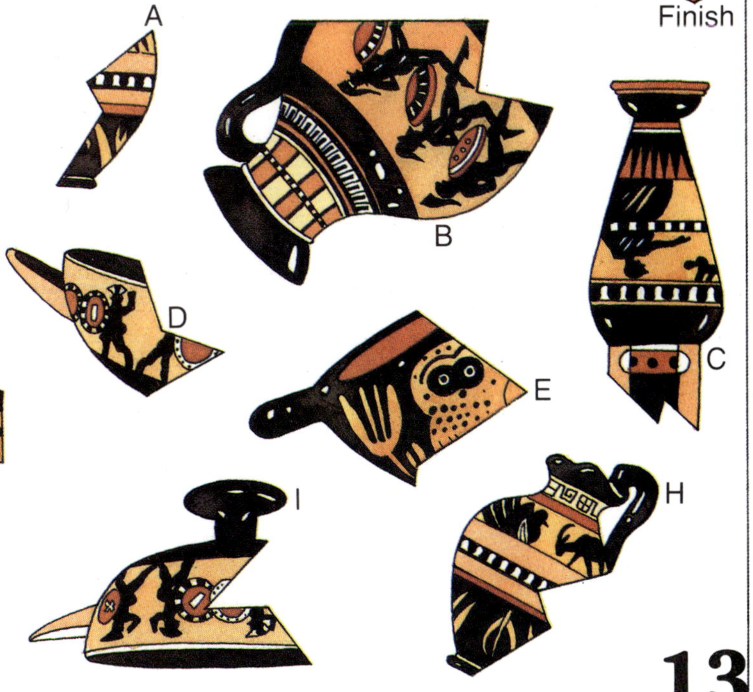

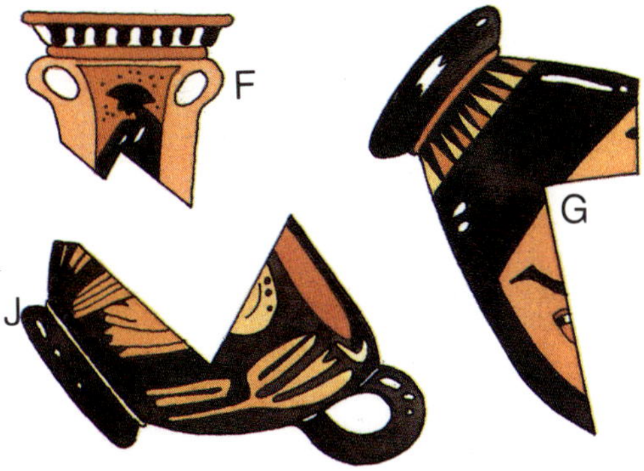

Solution: AH; BG; CF; DI; EJ

On Mount Olympus

Most Greeks belong to the Orthodox Church whose priests are called 'popes'. They wear long black gowns, long beards and flat-topped round hats. The churches shimmer with gold and candle-light and are richly decorated with pictures of the saints, called ikons. It's your turn to finish this ikon in the most glorious colours.

In Ancient Greece, however, the religion was totally different. There were numerous gods and goddesses who lived like a large family on Mount Olympus. Greek mythology is full of their adventures. They are often represented with their own special symbol. Here are the most important members of the dynasty. Can you return the right symbol to each of them?

Solution: A2; B8; C7; D6; E1; F5; G3; H4

Island hopping

Caiques are small fishing boats which are just right for discovering the islands.

This island race is a game for two.

1. Cut out the caiques and hands opposite.

2. Each player chooses two caiques of different colours and places them on the right colour track.

3. You take it in turns to hide the hands behind your back and ask your partner to pick one.

4. With a right hand, the boat on the right moves to the next square, with a left hand, the boat on the left moves on. If a player can't go any further, he misses a round.

5. You win the race if both boats have reached their destination.

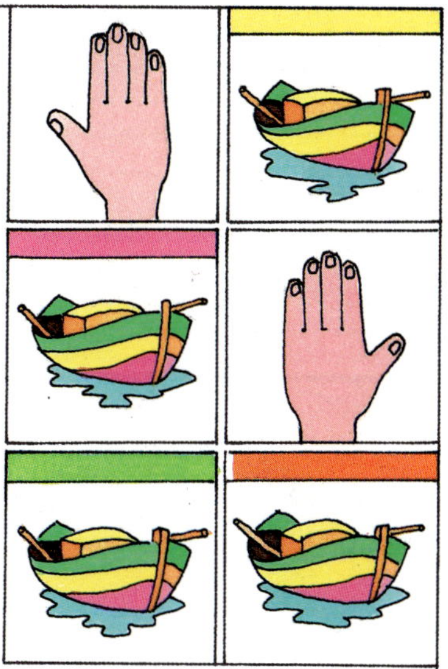

Samothrace
Kalymnos
Skopelos
Santorin
Corfu
Naxos

Let's dance!

The sound of the bouzouki and the traditional dances are very lively. Sometimes the spectators get so carried away that they throw plates onto the stage to express their enthusiasm! What missing instrument is the musician in our picture playing?

Solution: the bouzouki

Look at the costumes in the picture and colour in the dancing couple.

Easter feast

Easter is the great event of the year. Children get busy painting eggs and rolling them down slopes. You too can create colourful Easter eggs.

Now spot the pairs
among all the eggs on these two pages . . .

Solution: AK; BV; CQ; DZ; EO; FP; GU; HJ; IL; MR; NY; SX; TW

Greek delights

The Greeks eat their meals later in the day than we do. But if you study the various dishes carefully, you'll probably guess what these meals are, so draw in the right clock hands.

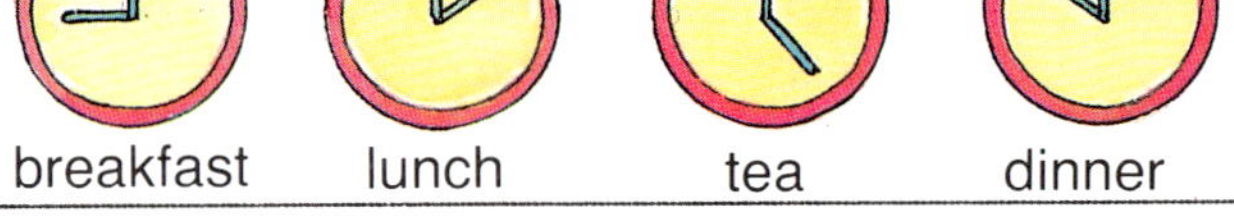

Solution: A=tea; B=lunch; C=breakfast; D=dinner

In the summer it gets very hot,
so meals always start with a
refreshing dish.

To prepare your own tsatsiki,
a cool cucumber salad, you need:
1 cucumber
fresh mint
olive oil
2 plain yoghurts
salt
Cut the cucumber into thin slices.
Sprinkle with salt.
Leave to drain in a bowl,
then dab dry.
Crush the mint leaves
in some olive oil.
Mix in the yoghurts.
Pour over the cucumber
and chill briefly.

Great Greeks

king and
conqueror

Look at these symbols:
they are also hidden in our pictures to help you find out
what each of these great men did.

doctor

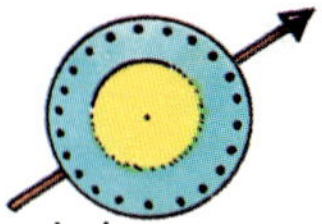
statesman

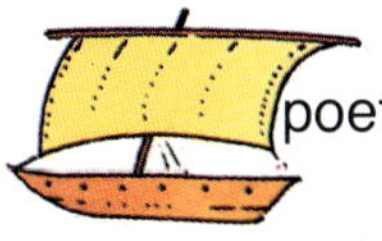
poet

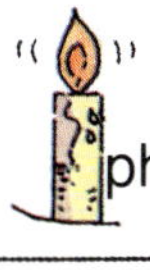
philosopher

mathematician

Solution: the philosopher Socrates had fresh, new ideas which appealed to young people. Homer is the author of the two epic poems Iliad and Odyssey. Pericles ruled over Athens. The empire of Alexander the Great stretched as far as India. Hippocrates became a shining example for all doctors. Pythagoras invented the multiplication table.

Sweet home . . .

There is more to Greece then ancient monuments: there are lavishly decorated orthodox churches, lots of windmills and bright blue and white houses. The men here have strayed into the wrong picture. Decide where each of them belongs. There is also something odd about each person . . . Can you spot it?

Solution: A2; B3; C1. The priest should have a beard. The miller is wearing cowboy boots. There are no oysters in Greece and you don't fish them with a net.

B
2
C
3

Holiday snaps

Here are some of my best pictures! They also make an exciting game. Each player throws a die in turn and moves along the board. The person who is the first to reach the photo of a caique, a pope, a bouzouki, a game of backgammon and a palace guard wins the game. You may move backwards or forward as you like. Make a list like this one and tick the pictures you have landed on.

3

4

5

8

7

6

15

16

17

20

19

18

Labour of Hercules

Hercules is the most famous of all Greek heroes. In his own country he is called Herakles. He is a sort of early Superman of prodigious strength. He is best known for the twelve extraordinary tasks he carried out.

Decide which is the right caption for each picture.

3. He managed to capture the Arcadian stag who had golden antlers and brass hooves.

1. No weapon could harm the cattle-killing Nemean lion . . . But Hercules strangled it with his bare hands.

6. The killer-birds of Lake Stymphalis were destroyed in their thousands by his poisoned arrows.

5. The Augean stables had never been cleaned: by moving some boulders, Hercules diverted an entire river through them.

8. He succeeded in taming the man-eating mares of Diomedes.

7. He caught the raging bull who had terrorised the people of Crete.

4. Using a net, he captured the monstrous Erymanthian boar alive.

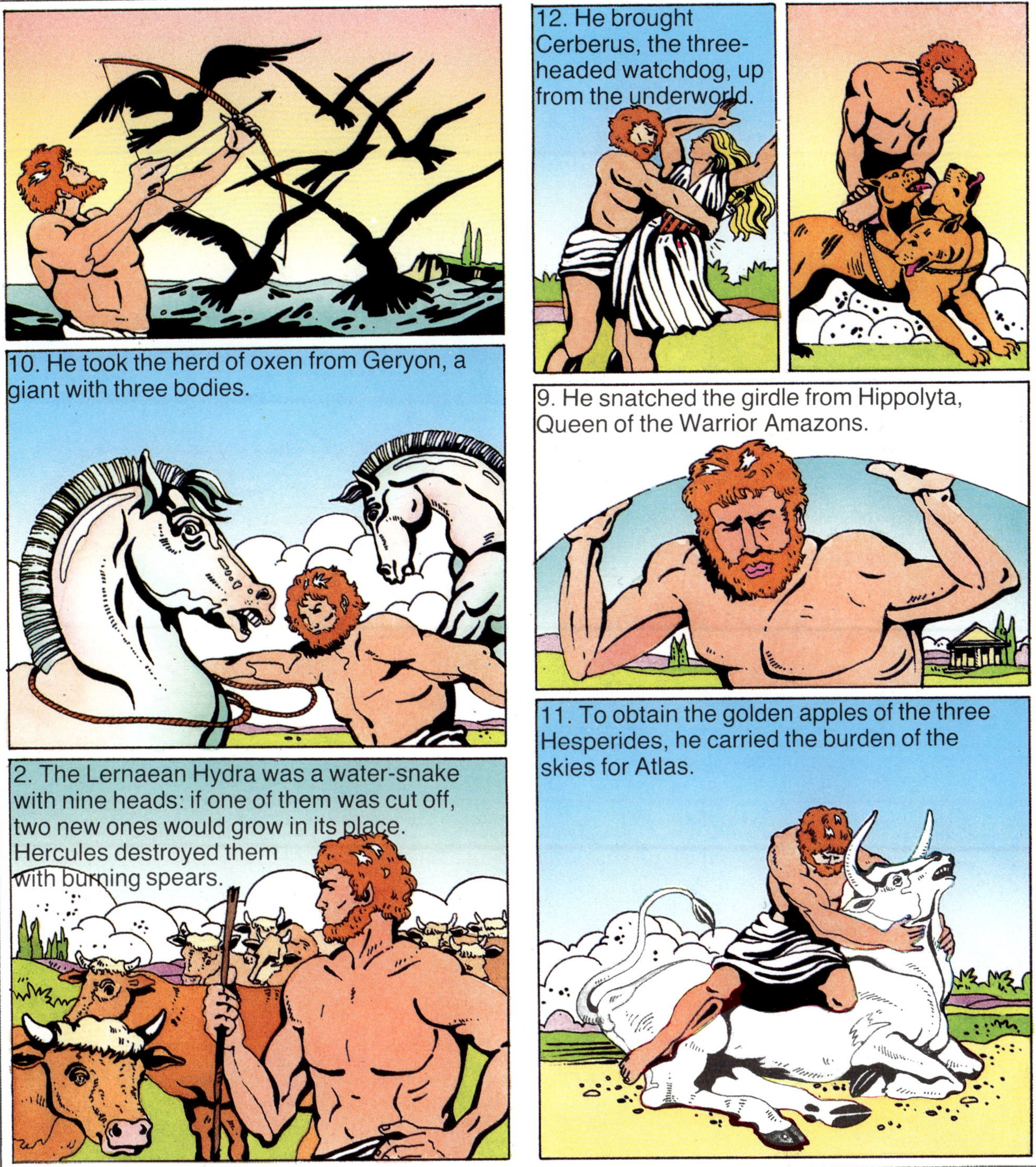

Puzzled by the maze?

Athens is the Greek capital.
Among its most famous ancient monuments
is the Temple of Parthenon
which sits on the hill of the Akropolis.

To get to the temple,
find your way out of this maze.
Follow the example of a Greek hero:
Theseus was the only one ever to escape
from the Cretan labyrinth . . . by simply
unrolling a thread to mark his way.

Imprimerie-Offset-Aubin, Poitiers — Dépôt légal nº 359-3-1986 (P 13884)
Collection nº 24 — Édition nº 91 — 24/1115/5
86-III